6 MEALS DIET
PLANS AND UNIQUE RECIPES

LOW-CARB PLANS AND RECIPES TO LOSE WEIGHT QUICKLY AND NATURALLY

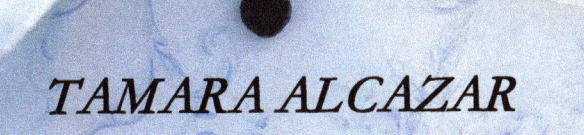

TAMARA ALCAZAR

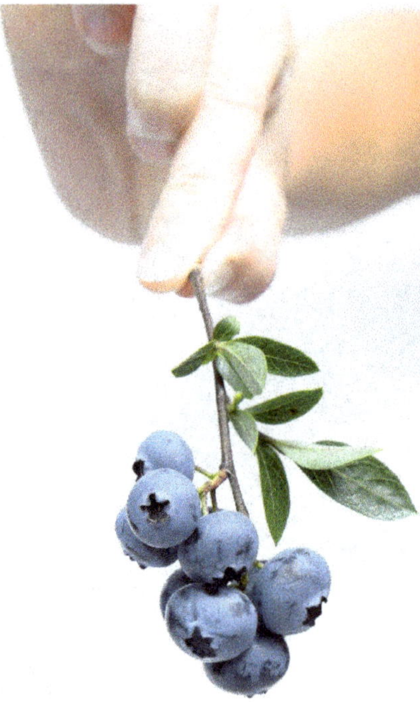

TABLE OF CONTENT

INTRODUCTION 12

WHAT 6 MEALS DIET CONSIST OF? 15

6 MEALS A DAY DIET PLANS 21

LEAN AND GREEN RECIPES 27
- SALMON FLORENTINE 29
- TOMATO BRAISED CAULIFLOWER WITH CHICKEN 31
- MEDITERRANEAN CHICKEN SALAD 33
- ORANGE SALAD 35
- RED PEPPER SALAD 36
- LIGHT RUSSIAN SALAD 37
- FETA SALAD 38
- GOAT CHEESE SALAD 39

FUELING RECIPES 41
- 6M FUELING MOUSSE 43
- BAKED CHEESY EGGPLANT 44
- TROPICAL GREENS SMOOTHIE 46
- VITAMIN C SMOOTHIE CUBES 47
- VANILLA BUCKWHEAT PORRIDGE 48

BREAKFAST RECIPES 49
- SWEET CASHEW CHEESE SPREAD 51
- PIZZA HACK 52
- MINI MAC IN A BOWL 54
- LEAN AND GREEN SMOOTHIE 56
- ALKALINE BLUEBERRY SPELT PANCAKES 57
- BANANA BARLEY PORRIDGE 58
- ZUCCHINI MUFFINS 59

MAINS 61
- RISOTTO WITH GREEN BEANS, SWEET POTATOES, AND PEAS 63
- MAPLE LEMON TEMPEH CUBES 64
- SIMPLE BEEF ROAST 66
- BAKED RICOTTA WITH PEARS 68
- CHICKEN BREAST SOUP 70
- MEDITERRANEAN BURRITO 71
- CHICKEN SALAD WITH PINEAPPLE AND PECANS 72

SNACKS RECIPES ... 73
- HUMMUS WITH GROUND LAMB ... 75
- WRAPPED PLUMS ... 76
- CHILI MANGO AND WATERMELON SALSA ... 77
- CREAMY SPINACH AND SHALLOTS DIP ... 78
- GOAT CHEESE AND CHIVES SPREAD ... 79
- MEDITERRANEAN CHICKEN SALAD ... 80
- LAMB STUFFED AVOCADO ... 82

VEGETABLES ... 85
- ASPARAGUS GREEN SCRAMBLE ... 87
- HEALTHY BROCCOLI SALAD ... 88
- CRISPY RYE BREAD SNACKS WITH GUACAMOLE AND ANCHOVIES ... 89
- MUSHROOMS STUFFED WITH TOMATO ... 90
- KALE SLAW AND STRAWBERRY SALAD + POPPYSEED DRESSING ... 92
- ROASTED ROOT VEGETABLES ... 94
- GRILLED EGGPLANTS ... 95

MEAT ... 97
- TURKEY TACO ... 99
- BRAISED COLLARD GREENS IN PEANUT SAUCE WITH PORK TENDERLOIN ... 100
- CHICKEN CRUST MARGHERITA PIZZA ... 102
- TOMATO STEAK ... 104
- TURKEY MEATBALLS ... 105
- ALMOND CUTLETS ... 106
- PORK SHANK WITH POTATO ... 108

SOUPS AND STEWS ... 111
- TOFU STIR FRY WITH ASPARAGUS ... 113
- CREAM OF THYME TOMATO SOUP ... 114
- SAVORY SPLIT PEA SOUP ... 115
- EASY FISH SOUP ... 116
- HOME MADE FISH BROTH ... 117
- ROMANIAN BEEF SOUP ... 118
- HOMEMADE BEEF BROTH ... 119
- ALL GREEN SOUPS ... 120

SMOOTHIES ... 121
- AVOCADO BLUEBERRY SMOOTHIE ... 123
- VEGAN BLUEBERRY SMOOTHIE ... 124
- REFRESHING CUCUMBER SMOOTHIE ... 125
- CAULIFLOWER VEGGIE SMOOTHIE ... 126
- PRICKLY PEAR JUICE ... 127

PROTEIC LIQUID CHOCOLATE 128
  BANANA YUMMY 129
  EXOTIC PASSION 130

DESSERTS 131
  NO BAKE FUELING PEANUT BUTTER BROWNIES 133
  CHOCOLATE BARS 134
  BLUEBERRY MUFFINS 135
  CHOCOLATE POPSICLE 136

CONCLUSION 137

© Copyright 2021 by Tamara Alcazar -All Rights Reserved.

The following Book is reproduced below with the goal of providing information that is as accurate and reliable as possible.

Regardless, purchasing this Book can be seen as consent to the fact that both the publisher and the author of this book are in no way experts on the topics discussed within and that any recommendations or suggestions that are made herein are for entertainment purposes only.

Professionals should be consulted as needed prior to undertaking any of the action endorsed herein.
This declaration is deemed fair and valid by both the American Bar Association and the Committee of Publishers Association and is legally binding throughout the United States.

Furthermore, the transmission, duplication, or reproduction of any of the following work including specific information will be considered an illegal act irrespective of if it is done electronically or in print. This extends to creating a secondary or tertiary copy of the work or a recorded copy and is only allowed with the express written consent from the Publisher. All additional right reserved.

The information in the following pages is broadly considered a truthful and accurate account of facts and as such, any inattention, use, or misuse of the information in question by the reader will render any resulting actions solely under their purview.
There are no scenarios in which the publisher or the original author of this work can be in any fashion deemed liable for any hardship or damages that may befall them after

undertaking information described herein.

Additionally, the information in the following pages is intended only for informational purposes and should thus be thought of as universal. As befitting its nature, it is presented without assurance regarding its prolonged validity or interim quality.

Trademarks that are mentioned are done without written consent and can in no way be considered an endorsement from the trademark holder.

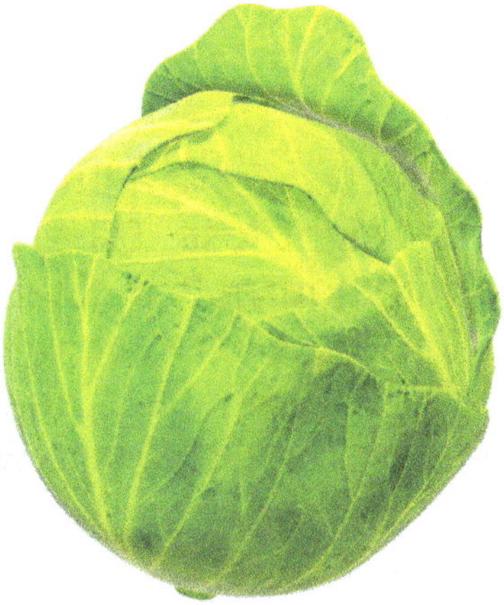

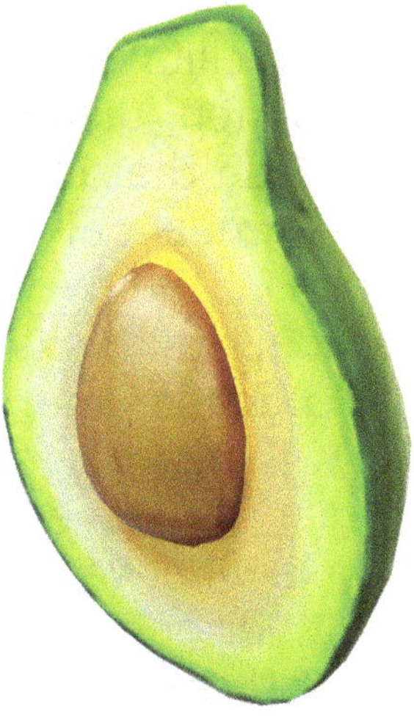

INTRODUCTION

The 6 Meals Diet has been subjected to various studies to Prove its efficacy in weight loss. Different studies were Published in various journals indicating that those who follow this Program are able to see significant changes in as little as 8 weeks and that People can achieve their long-term health goals with this Diet.
While the initial 5&1 ideal weight Plan is quite restrictive, maintenance.
Phases 3&3 allow for greater variety of less Processed foods and
snacks, which can facilitate weight loss.
Under this diet regimen, dieters are required to follow a weight Plan that includes five fueling a day and one lean green meal daily. However, there are also other regimens if the five meals a day is too much for you. And since this is a commercial diet, you have access to coaches and become Part of a community that will encourage you to succeed in your weight loss journey. Moreover, this diet is also designed for people who want to transition from their old habits to healthier ones.
The diet is a set of three Programs, two of which focus on weight loss and one that is best for weight maintenance, if you are not trying to lose weight. The Plans are high in Protein and low in carbohydrates and calories to stimulate weight loss. Each Program requires you to eat at least half of the food in the form of numerous healthy Prepackaged foods.
Since the Plan requires the intake of carbohydrates, Protein and fat, it is also a relatively balanced Plan when it comes to food Groups.

When it comes to weight loss, Experts say that while 6 Meals Can help because it is essentially less caloric, it is unlikely to Improve your eating habits Permanently. You are more likely to gain weight after Stopping the diet.

Also, diet Experts warn that this Pattern may not contain enough calories to meet your body's needs. "In terms of overall health and nutrition, as well as convenience, this diet isn't at the Top of my list of best approaches." she says.

If you are interested in trying this, consider working with an experienced registered dietitian who can help you stay properly fed as you strive to achieve your desired weight.

For the most desirable 5 and 1 weight Plan, eat 5 foods Per day, Plus a low carb lean meal and a low carb elective snack.

Although Initial Plan 5 & 1 is reasonably restrictive, Protection Segment 3 & 3 allows for a greater variety of less Processed foods and snacks, which can also make weight loss easier and more Persistent for long Period.

The bottom line is, that the 6 Meals weight loss Plan Promotes weight loss via low calorie prepackaged meals; low carb homemade food, and Personalized coaching; at the same time, as this system Promotes quick-time Period weight and fat loss, similarly research is wanted to assess whether it encourages the everlasting way of life adjustments needed for long-time Period achievement.

WHAT 6 MEALS DIET CONSIST OF?

The 6 Meals diet is a Practice that aims to reduce or maintain current weight. It is a diet that recommends eating a combination of processed foods called fueling and home-cooked meals (lean and green meals). It is believed that it sticks to the brand Product (Input) and supplements it with meat, vegetables, and fatty snacks; this will keep you satisfied and nourished.

At the same time you don't need to worry much about losing muscles because you are eating enough Protein and consuming too few calories.

And that way, the individual who Practices the diet can lose around 12 Pounds in just 12 weeks using the ideal 5&1 weight Plan.

In short, the 6 Meals diet is a Program that focuses on cutting calories and reducing carbohydrates in meals. To do this effectively, combine Packaged foods called fuels with home-cooked meals, which encourages weight loss.

Like many commercial Plans, this diet involves buying most of the foods Permitted on a diet in Packaged form. The company deals on a wide range of food Products. These include Pancakes, shakes, Pasta dishes, soups, cookies, mashed Potatoes, and Popcorns.

Users Pick the Plan that best suits them. The 5 & 1 Plan entails eating five small meals Per day. The meals can be selected from more than 60 substitutable fueling, including one "lean and green" meal, probably veggies or protein that you will Prepare by yourself.

A flexible Option is the 4 & 2 & 1 Plan. It just contains four Supplies a day; you can choose and create two of your "lean and green" meals and one of the protein snacks .

The Program is already Present in the '80s and '90s with doctors who Prescribe meals to their clients. This diet makes use of identical foods with a similar macronutrient Profile. Consumers can sign up online for the Plan by themselves.

How Much Does 6 Meals Diet Cost?

In comparison, the United States Departments of Agriculture estimates that a woman whose ages range from 10-50 can follow a nutritious diet while spending as little as $166.40 Per month on groceries. As long as she is preparing all her meals at home.

	Optimal Weight 5&1 Plan	Federal Government Recommendation
Calories	800-1,000	Men 19-25: 2,800 26-45: 2,600 46-65: 2,400 65+: 2,200 Women 19-25: 2,200 26-50: 2,000 51+: 1,800
Total fat % of Calorie Intake	20%	20%-35%
Total Carbohydrates % of Calorie Intake	40%	45%-65%
Sugars	10%-20%	N/A
Fiber	25 g – 30 g	Men 19-30: 34 g. 31-50: 31 g. 51+: 28 g. Women 19-30: 28 g. 31-50: 25 g. 51+: 22 g.
Protein	40%	10%-35%

Sodium	Under 2,300 mg	Under 2,300 mg.
Potassium	Average 3,000 mg	At least 4,700 mg.
Calcium	1,000 mg – 1,200 mg	Men 1,000 mg. Women 19-50: 1,000 mg. 51+: 1,200 mg.

6 MEALS A DAY DIET PLANS

The 6 Meals Diet encourages people to limit the number of calories that they should take daily. Under this Program, dieters are encouraged to consume between 800 and 1000 calories daily. For this to be Possible, dieters are encouraged to oPt for healthier food items as well as meal replacements. But unlike other types of commercial diet regimens, the 6 Meals Diet comes in different variations. There are currently three variations of Diet Plans that one can choose from according to one's needs.

- 5&1 Diet Plan: This is the most common version, and it involves eating five Prepackaged meals from the Health Fueling and one home-made balanced meal.

- 4&2&1 Diet Plan: This diet Plan is designed for people who want to have flexibility while following this regimen. Under this Program, dieters are encouraged to eat more calories and have more flexible food choices. This means that they can consume 4 prepackaged optimal Health Fuels food, three home-cooked meals from the Lean and Green, and one snack daily.

- 5&2&2 Diet Plan: This diet Plan is Perfect for individuals who Prefer to have a flexible meal Plan in order to achieve a healthy weight. It is recommended for a wide variety of people. Under this diet regimen, dieters are required to eat 5 fuels, 2 lean and green meals, and 2 healthy snacks.
- 3&3 Diet Plan: This Particular Diet Plan is created for people who have moderate weight Problems and merely want to maintain a healthy body. Under this diet Plan,

dieters are encouraged to consume 3 prepackaged optimal Health Fuels and three home-cooked meals.

- 6 Meals Diet for Nursing Mothers: This diet regimen is designed for nursing mothers with babies of at least two months old. Aside from supporting breastfeeding mothers, it also encourages gradual weight loss.

- 6 Meals for Diabetes: This Diet Plan is designed for people who have Type 1 and Type 2 diabetes. The meal Plans are designed so that dieters consume more green and lean meals, depending on their needs and condition.

- 6 Meals for Gout: This diet regimen incorporates a balance of foods that are low in Purines and moderate in Protein.

- 6 Meals for Seniors (65 years and older): Designed for seniors, this Diet Plan has some variations following the components of Fuels depending on the needs and activities of the senior dieters.

- 6 Meals for Teen Boys and Girls (13-18 years old): Designed for active teens, the 6 Meals for Teens Boys and 6 meals for Teens Girls Provide the right nutrition to growing teens.

- Regardless of which type of 6 Meals Diet Plan

How to Start This Diet

The 6 Meals Diet is comprised of different Phases. A certified coach will educate you on the steps that you need to undertake if you want to follow this regimen., below are some the things you need to know, especially when you are still starting with this diet regimen.

Initial Steps

During this phase, people are encouraged to consume800 to 1,000 calories to help you shed off at least 12 Pounds within the next 12 weeks. For instance, if you are following the 5&1 Diet Plan, then you need to eat 1 meal every 2 or 3 hours and include a 30-minute moderate workout most days of your week. You need to consume not more than 100 grams of Carbs daily during this Phase.

<u>Further, consuming meals are highly encouraged.</u>

This Phase also encourages the dieter to include 1 optional snack Per day, such as ½ cup sugar-free gelatin, 3 celery sticks, and 12 ounces nuts. Aside from these things, below are other things that you need to remember when following this Phase:

- Make sure that the Portion size recommendations are for cooked weight and not the raw weight of your ingredients

- Opt for meals that are baked, grilled, broiled, or poached. Avoid frying foods, as this will increase your calorie intake.

- Eat at least 2 servings of fish rich in Omega-3 fatty acids. These include fishes like tuna, salmon, trout, mackerel, herring, and other cold-water fishes.

- Choose meatless alternatives like tofu and Tempeh.

- Follow the Program even when you are dining out. Keep in mind that drinking alcohol is discouraged when following this Plan.

Maintenance Phase

As soon as you have attained your desired weight, the next Phase is the transition stage.
It is a 6-week stage that involves increasing your calorie intake to 1,550 Per day. This is also the Phase when you are allowed to add more varieties into your meal, such as whole grains, low-fat dairy, and fruits.
After six weeks, you can now move into the 3&3 Diet Plan, so you are required to eat three Lean and Green meals and 3 Fuels foods.

LEAN AND GREEN RECIPES

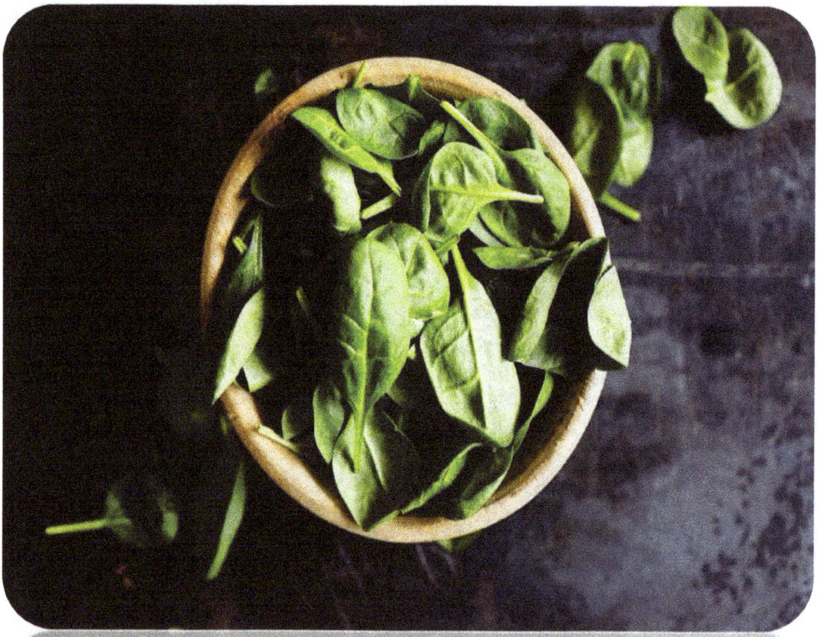

SALMON FLORENTINE

COOKING: 30' PREPARATION: 5' SERVES: 4

INGREDIENTS

- ½ cups of chopped cherry tomatoes
- ½ cup of chopped green onions
- garlic cloves, minced
- teaspoon of olive oil
- quantity of 12 oz. package frozen chopped spinach, thawed and patted dry
- ¼ teaspoon of crushed red pepper flakes
- ½ cup of part-skim ricotta cheese
- ¼ teaspoon each for pepper and salt
- quantities of 5 ½ oz. wild salmon fillets
- Cooking spray

DIRECTIONS

1. Preheat the oven to 3500F
2. Get a medium skillet to cook onions in oil until they start to soften, which should be in about 2 minutes. You can then add garlic inside the skillet and cook for an extra 1 minute. Add the spinach, red pepper flakes, tomatoes, pepper, and salt. Cook for 2 minutes while stirring. Remove the pan from the heat and let it cool for about 10 minutes. Stir in the ricotta.
3. Put a quarter of the spinach mixture on top of each salmon fillet. Place the fillets on a slightly greased rimmed baking sheet and bake it for 15 minutes or until you are sure that the salmon has been thoroughly cooked.

NUTRITIONS: Calories: 350 Carbohydrate: 15 g
Protein: 42 g Fat: 13 g

TOMATO BRAISED CAULIFLOWER WITH CHICKEN

COOKING: 30' PREPARATION: 10' SERVES: 4

INGREDIENTS

- 4 garlic cloves, sliced
- 3 scallions, to be trimmed and cut into 1-inch pieces
- ¼ teaspoon of dried oregano
- ¼ teaspoon of crushed red pepper flakes
- 4 ½ cups of cauliflower
- 1 ½ cups of diced canned tomatoes
- 1 cup of fresh basil, gently torn
- ½ teaspoon each of pepper and salt, divided
- 1 ½ teaspoon of olive oil
- 1 ½ lb. of boneless, skinless chicken breasts

DIRECTIONS

1. Get a saucepan and combine the garlic, scallions, oregano, crushed red pepper, cauliflower, and tomato, and add ¼ cup of water. Get everything boil together and add ¼ teaspoon of pepper and salt for seasoning, then cover the pot with a lid. Let it simmer for 10 minutes and stir as often as possible until you observe that the cauliflower is tender. Now, wrap up the seasoning with the remaining ¼ teaspoon of pepper and salt.
2. Toss the chicken breast with oil, olive preferably and let it roast in the oven with the heat of 4500F for 20 minutes and an internal temperature of 1650F. Allow the chicken to rest for like 10 minutes.
3. Now slice the chicken, and serve on a bed of tomato

braised cauliflower.

NUTRITIONS: Calories: 290 Fat: 10 g Carbohydrate: 13 g Protein: 38 g

MEDITERRANEAN CHICKEN SALAD

COOKING: 25' PREPARATION: 5' SERVES: 4

INGREDIENTS

» For Chicken:
» 1 ¾ lb. boneless, skinless chicken breast
» ¼ teaspoon each of pepper and salt (or as desired)
» 1 ½ tablespoon of butter, melted
» For Mediterranean salad:
» 1 cup of sliced cucumber
» 6 cups of romaine lettuce, that is torn or roughly chopped
» 10 pitted Kalamata olives
» 1 pint of cherry tomatoes
» 1/3 cup of reduced-fat feta cheese
» ¼ teaspoon each of pepper and salt (or lesser)
» 1 small lemon juice (it should be about 2 tablespoons)

DIRECTIONS

1. Preheat your oven or grill to about 3500F.
2. Season the chicken with salt, butter, and black pep- per
3. Roast or grill chicken until it reaches an internal temperature of 1650F in about 25 minutes. Once your chicken breasts are cooked, remove and keep aside to rest for about 5 minutes before you slice it.
4. Combine all the salad ingredients you have and toss
everything together very well
5. Serve the chicken with Mediterranean salad

NUTRITIONS: Calories: 290 Fat: 10 g Carbohydrate: 13 g Protein: 38 g

ORANGE SALAD

COOKING: 0 PREPARATION: 5m SERVES: 4

INGREDIENTS

- 2 fennel bulbs
- 5 blood oranges
- 2 red onion
- Fine olive oil
- Fine balsamic vinegar (Optional)
- Salt and black pepper to taste

DIRECTIONS

The best way to serve orange salad and in a flat dish the size of pizza.
Peel and cut the oranges first into slices for, and then divide the slices into four wedges,
Repeat the same process for all oranges and place them on the plate to create a base.
Cut the onions first in half and then in very thin slices. The same for fennel.
Season it all and Enjoy!

NUTRITIONS: Calories: 270 Cal Fats: 7 g Carbohydrates: 3g Protein: 5g

RED PEPPER SALAD

COOKING: 0 PREPARATION: 5m SERVES: 4

INGREDIENTS

- 3 Red peppers
- 2 bunches of arugula
- 20 cherry tomato
- 1 red onion
- 20 black olives
- 3 spoon olive oil
- 1 spoon balsamic vinegar (Optional)
- Salt and pepper to taste

DIRECTIONS

Wash the peppers, cut them in half and remove the seeds.
Cut them into small pieces, chop the onion, tag the tomatoes in half and mixture everything together with the arugula.
Season and enjoy!

NUTRITIONS: Calories: 230 Cal Fats: 3 g Carbohydrates: 3g Protein: 7g

LIGHT RUSSIAN SALAD

COOKING: 0 PREPARATION: 5m SERVES: 4

INGREDIENTS

- 4 boiled egg
- 200g ready to eat peas
- 100g boiled and chopped carrots
- 200g Greek yogurt 0% fat
- 3 spoon olive oil
- 30g Russian mustard (Optional)
- Chopped coriander to taste
- Salt and pepper to taste

DIRECTIONS

Cut the boiled eggs in little pieces , and put them in a salad-bowl.
Add the rest of the ingredients and mix well.
Let it chill in the fridge for more than 30 minutes.
Enjoy!

NUTRITIONS: Calories: 310 Cal Fats: 4 g
Carbohydrates: 5g Protein: 12g

FETA SALAD

COOKING: 0 PREPARATION: 5m SERVES: 2

INGREDIENTS

- 70g feta cheese
- 100g pomegranate grains
- 2 Hand full of spinach leaf
- 2 spoons of Olive oil
- 1 spoon Balsamic vinegar
- Salt and pepper to taste

DIRECTIONS

Cut the feta cheese into little pieces and put in a salad bowl along with the rest of the ingredients.
Season and Enjoy!

NUTRITIONS: Calories: 550g Cal Fats: 5 g Carbohydrates: 5g Protein: 8g

GOAT CHEESE SALAD

COOKING: 0 PREPARATION: 5m SERVES: 2

INGREDIENTS

- 60g goat cheese
- 70g red grapes
- 40g beetroot
- 2 Hand full of spinach
- 1 hand full of rocket
- 2 spoon olive oil
- 1 spoon balsamic vinegar
- Salt and pepper to taste

DIRECTIONS

Cut the goat cheese into tiny cubes with a hot knife.
Cut the red grapes in half.
Put all the ingredients that you prepared before in a salad bowl and mix well.
Season and enjoy!

NUTRITIONS:
Calories: 650 Cal Fats: 15 g Carbohydrates: 14g Protein: 18g

FUELING RECIPES

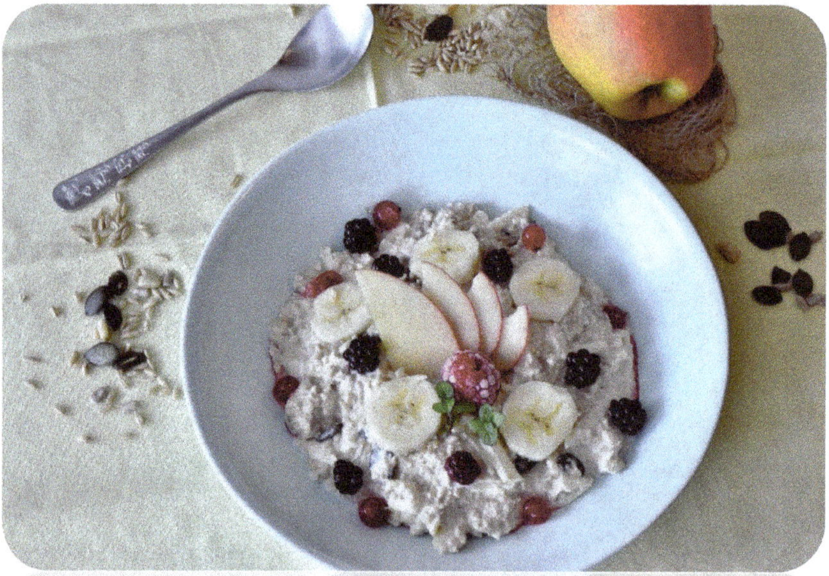

6M FUELING MOUSSE

COOKING: 3' PREPARATION: 3' SERVES: 2

INGREDIENTS

- 1 packet hot cocoa
- 1/2 cup sugar-free gelatin
- 1 tablespoon light cream cheese
- 2 tablespoons cold water
- 1/4 cup crushed ice

DIRECTIONS

1. Place all ingredients in a blender.
2. Pulse until smooth.
3. Pour into glass and place in the fridge to set.
4. Serve chilled.

NUTRITIONS: Calories per serving: 156 Cal Protein: 5.7 g Carbs: 17.6 g Fat: 3.7 g Sugar:4.5 g

BAKED CHEESY EGGPLANT

COOKING: 1 H 15' PREPARATION: 20' SERVES: 6

INGREDIENTS

- Eggplant (1, fresh)
- Tomato (1, 16 can, chopped)
- Tomato sauce (2, 8 oz. can)
- Cheddar cheese (6 oz., shredded)
- Onion (1, chopped)
- Oregano (dash, dried)
- Salt (2 tsp.)
- Italian seasoning (dash)
- Basil (dried, for taste)
- Thyme (dried, for flavor)
- Garlic (2-3 tsp., powdered)
- Black pepper (1/2 tsp.)

DIRECTIONS

1. Slice eggplant (fresh) into thin slices then season
using a dash of salt.
2. Next, set aside in a colander for roughly 30 minutes
then pat dry using a few paper towels.
3. Rinse under warm running water and thoroughly slice eggplant into quarters.
4. Place a layer of the eggplant (quartered) into a baking dish (large).
5. Cover layer using the tomatoes (chopped) and tomato sauce (1 can).

6. Add 1/2 of the cheese over the top and repeat layers with the remaining cheese (shredded) over the top.
7. Place eggplant into the oven to bake for approximately 45 minutes at 350 degrees Fahrenheit until eggplant is soft.

NUTRITIONS: Protein: 11.7 g Carbohydrates: 15.4 g Dietary Fiber: 5.4 g

TROPICAL GREENS SMOOTHIE

COOKING: 0' PREPARATION: 5' SERVES: 1

INGREDIENTS
- One banana
- 1/2 large navel orange, peeled and segmented
- 1/2 cup frozen mango chunks
- 1 cup frozen spinach
- One celery stalk, broken into pieces
- One tablespoon cashew butter or almond butter
- 1/2 tablespoon spiraling
- 1/2 tablespoon ground flaxseed
- 1/2 cup unsweetened nondairy milk
- Water, for thinning (optional)

DIRECTIONS
1. In a high-speed blender or food processor, combine the bananas, orange, mango, spinach, celery, cashew butter, spiraling (if using), flaxseed, and milk.
2. Blend until creamy, adding more milk or water to thin the smoothie if too thick. Serve immediately—it is best served fresh.

NUTRITIONS: Calories: 391 Fat: 12g Protein: 13g Carbohydrates: 68g Fiber: 13g

VITAMIN C SMOOTHIE CUBES

COOKING: 1H TO CHILL INGREDIENTS
PREPARATION: 5' SERVES: 1

INGREDIENTS
- » 1/8 large papaya
- » 1/8 mango
- » 1/4 cups chopped pineapple, fresh or frozen
- » 1/8 cup raw cauliflower florets, fresh or frozen
- » 1/4 large navel oranges, peeled and halved
- » 1/4 large orange bell pepper stemmed, seeded, and coarsely chopped.

DIRECTIONS
1. Halve the papaya and mango, remove the pits, and scoop their soft flesh into a high-speed blender.
2. Add the pineapple, cauliflower, oranges, and bell pepper. Blend until smooth.
3. Evenly divide the puree between 2 (16-compartment) ice cube trays and place them on a level sur- face in your freezer. Freeze for at least 8 hours.
4. The cubes can be left in the ice cube trays until use or transferred to a freezer bag. The frozen cubes are good for about three weeks in a standard freezer or up to 6 months in a chest freezer.

NUTRITIONS: Calories: 96 Fat: <1g Protein: 2g Carbohydrates: 24g Fiber: 4g

VANILLA BUCKWHEAT PORRIDGE

COOKING: 25' PREPARATION: 5' SERVES: 1

INGREDIENTS
- One cup of water
- 1/4 cup raw buckwheat grouts
- 1/4 teaspoon ground cinnamon
- 1/4 banana, sliced
- 1/16 cup golden raisins
- 1/16 cup dried currants
- 1/16 cup sunflower seeds
- 1/2 tablespoons chia seeds
- 1/4 tablespoon hemp seed
- 1/4 tablespoon sesame seed, toasted
- 1/8 cup unsweetened nondairy milk
- 1/4 tablespoon pure maple syrup
- 1/4 teaspoon vanilla extract

DIRECTIONS
1. Boil the water in a pot. Stir in the buckwheat, cinnamon, and banana. Cook the mixture. Mixing it and wait for it to boil, then reduce the heat to medium-low. Cover the pot and cook for 15 minutes, or
until the buckwheat is tender. Remove from the heat.
2. Stir in the raisins, currants, sunflower seeds, chia seeds, hemp seeds, sesame seeds, milk, maple syrup, and vanilla. Cover the pot. Wait for 10 minutes be- fore serving.
3. Serve as is or top as desired.

NUTRITIONS: Calories: 353 Fat: 11g Protein: 10g Carbohydrates: 61g Fiber: 10g

BREAKFAST RECIPES

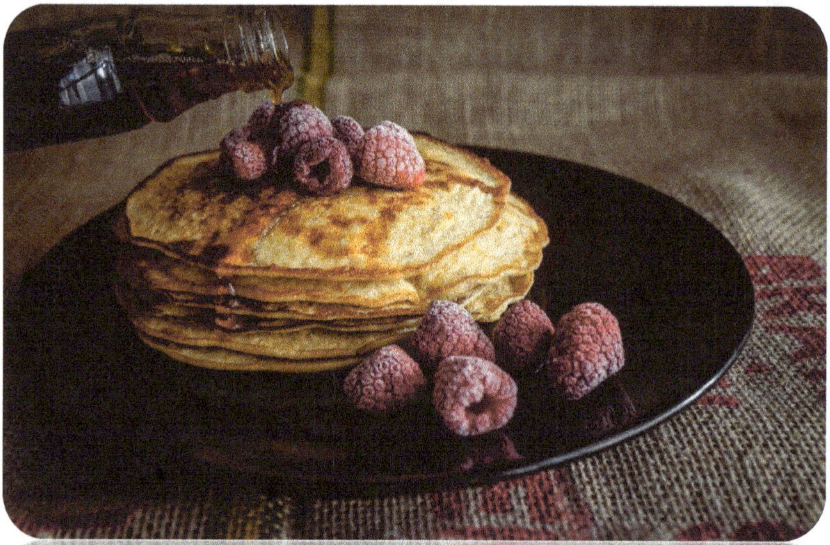

SWEET CASHEW CHEESE SPREAD

COOKING: 5'   PREPARATION: 5' SERVES: 10

INGREDIENTS
- Stevia (5 drops)
- Cashews (2 cups, raw)
- Water (1/2 cup)

DIRECTIONS
1. Soak the cashews overnight in water.
2. Next, drain the excess water then transfer cashews toa food processor.
3. Add in the stevia and the water.
4. Process until smooth.
5. Serve chilled. Enjoy.

NUTRITIONS: Fat: 7 g Cholesterol 0 mg Sodium 12.6 mg Carbohydrates 5.7 g

PIZZA HACK

COOKING: 15-20' PREPARATION: 5-10' SERVES: 1

INGREDIENTS
» 1/4 fueling of garlic mashed potato
» 1/2 egg whites
» 1/4 tablespoon of Baking powder
» 3/4 oz. of reduced-fat shredded mozzarella
» 1/8 cup of sliced white mushrooms
» 1/16 cup of pizza sauce
» 3/4 oz. of ground beef
» 1/4 sliced black olives
» You also need a sauté pan, baking sheets, and parchment paper

DIRECTIONS
1. Start by preheating the oven to 400°
2. Mix your baking powder and garlic potato packet
3. Add egg whites to your mixture and stir well until it
blends.
4. Line the baking sheet with parchment paper and pour the mixed batter onto it
5. Put another parchment paper on top of the batter
and spread out the batter to a 1/8-inch circle.
6. Then place another baking sheet on top; this way,
the matter is between two baking sheets.
7. Place into an oven and bake for about 8 minutes until the pizza crust is golden brown.
8. For the toppings, place your ground beef in a sauté pan and fry till its brown, and wash your mushrooms very well.

9. After the crust is baked, remove the top layer of parchment paper carefully to prevent the form from sticking to the pizza crust.
10. Put your toppings on top of the crust and bake for
an extra 8 minutes.
11. Once ready, slide the pizza off the parchment paper
and into a plate.

NUTRITIONS: Calories: 478 Protein: 30 g Carbohydrates: 22 g Fats: 29 g

MINI MAC IN A BOWL

COOKING: 15' PREPARATION: 5' SERVES: 1

INGREDIENTS
- 5 ounce of lean ground beef
- Two tablespoons of diced white or yellow onion.
- 1/8 teaspoon of onion powder
- 1/8 teaspoon of white vinegar
- 1 ounce of dill pickle slices
- One teaspoon sesame seed
- 3 cups of shredded Romaine lettuce
- Cooking spray
- Two tablespoons reduced-fat shredded cheddar cheese
- Two tablespoons of Wish-bone light thousand island as dressing

DIRECTIONS
1. Place a lightly greased small skillet on fire to heat,
2. Add your onion to cook for about 2-3 minutes,
3. Next, add the beef and allow cooking until it's brown
4. Next, mix your vinegar and onion powder with the dressing,
5. Finally, top the lettuce with the cooked meat and sprinkle cheese on it, add your pickle slices.
6. Drizzle the mixture with the sauce and sprinkle the sesame seeds also.
7. Your mini mac in a bowl is ready for consumption.

NUTRITIONS: Calories: 150 Protein: 21 g Carbohydrates: 32 g Fats: 19 g

LEAN AND GREEN SMOOTHIE

COOKING: 5' PREPARATION: 0 SERVES: 1

INGREDIENTS

- 2 1/2 cups of kale leaves
- 3/4 cup of chilled apple juice
- 1 cup of cubed pineapple
- 1/2 cup of frozen green grapes
- 1/2 cup of chopped apple

DIRECTIONS

1. Place the pineapple, apple juice, apple, frozen seed- less grapes, and kale leaves in a blender.
2. Cover and blend until it's smooth.
3. Smoothie is ready and can be garnished with halved
grapes if you wish.

NUTRITIONS: Calories: 8 Protein: 2 g Carbohydrates: 10 g Fat: 1 g

ALKALINE BLUEBERRY SPELT PANCAKES

COOKING: 20' PREPARATION: 6' SERVES: 3

INGREDIENTS

- 2 cups Spelt Flour
- 1 cup Coconut Milk
- 1/2 cup Alkaline Water
- 2 tbsps. Grapeseed Oil
- 1/2 cup Agave
- 1/2 cup Blueberries
- 1/4 tsp. Sea Moss

DIRECTIONS

1. Mix the spelt flour, agave, grapeseed oil, hemp seeds,
and the sea moss together in a bowl.
2. Add in 1 cup of hemp milk and alkaline water to the mixture, until you get the consistency mixture you like.
3. Crimp the blueberries into the batter.
4. Heat the skillet to moderate heat then lightly coat it with the grapeseed oil.
5. Pour the batter into the skillet then let them cook for
approximately 5 minutes on every side.
6. Serve and Enjoy.

NUTRITIONS: Calories: 203 kcal Fat: 1.4g Carbs: 41.6g Proteins: 4.8g

BANANA BARLEY PORRIDGE

COOKING: 5' PREPARATION: 15' SERVES: 2

INGREDIENTS
- 1 cup divided unsweetened coconut milk
- 1 small peeled and sliced banana
- 1/2 cup barley
- 3 drops liquid stevia
- 1/4 cup chopped coconuts

DIRECTIONS
1. In a bowl, properly mix barley with half of the coco- nut milk and stevia.
2. Cover the mixing bowl then refrigerate for about 6 hours.
3. In a saucepan, mix the barley mixture with coconut milk.
4. Cook for about 5 minutes on moderate heat.
5. Then top it with the chopped coconuts and the ba- nana slices.
6. Serve.

NUTRITIONS: Calories: 159kcal Fat: 8.4g Carbs: 19.8g Proteins: 4.6g

ZUCCHINI MUFFINS

COOKING: 25' PREPARATION: 10 'SERVES:16

INGREDIENTS
- 1 tbsp. ground flaxseed
- 3 tbsps. alkaline water
- 1/4 cup walnut butter
- 3 medium over-ripe bananas
- 2 small, grated zucchinis
- 1/2 cup coconut milk
- 1 tsp. vanilla extract
- 2 cups coconut flour
- 1 tbsp. baking powder
- 1 tsp. cinnamon
- 1/4 tsp. sea salt

DIRECTIONS
1. Tune the temperature of your oven to 375ºF.
2. Grease the muffin tray with the cooking spray.
3. In a bowl, mix the flaxseed with water.
4. In a glass bowl, mash the bananas then stir in the remaining ingredients.
5. Properly mix and then divide the mixture into the muffin tray.
6. Bake it for 25 minutes.
7. Serve.

NUTRITIONS: Calories: 127 kcal Fat: 6.6g Carbs: 13g Protein: 0.7g

MAINS

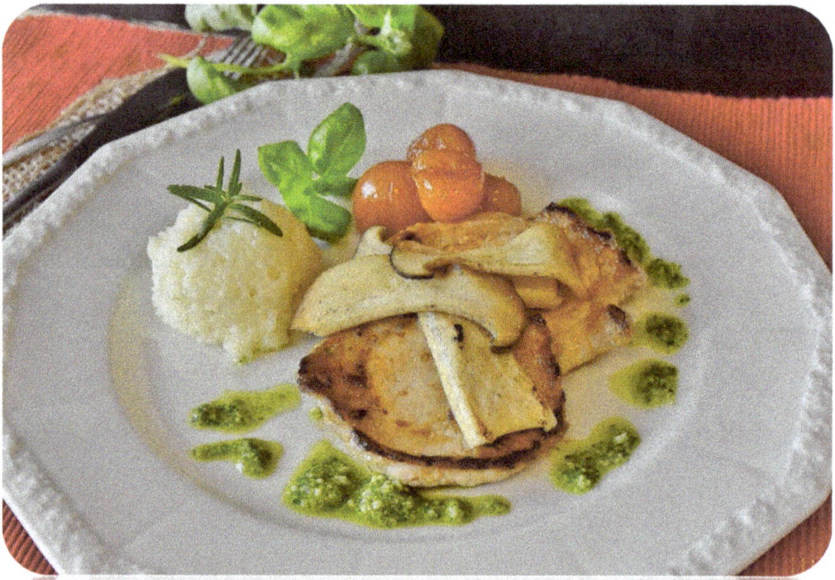

RISOTTO WITH GREEN BEANS, SWEET POTATOES, AND PEAS

COOKING: 4-5H PREPARATION: 20' SERVES: 8

INGREDIENTS
- 1 large sweet potato, peeled and chopped
- 1 onion, chopped
- 5 garlic cloves, minced
- 2 cups short-grain brown rice
- 1 teaspoon dried thyme leaves
- 7 cups low-sodium vegetable broth
- 2 cups green beans, cut in half crosswise
- 2 cups frozen baby peas
- 3 tablespoons unsalted butter
- 1/2 cup grated Parmesan cheese

DIRECTIONS
1. In a 6-quart slow cooker, mix the sweet potato, on- ion, garlic, rice, thyme, and broth.
2. Cover and cook on low for 3 to 4 hours, or until the rice is tender.
3. Stir in the green beans and frozen peas.
4. Cover and cook on low for 30 to 40 minutes or until the vegetables are tender.
5. Stir in the butter and cheese. Cover and cook on low for 20 minutes, then stir and serve.

NUTRITIONS: Calories: 385 Cal Carbohydrates: 52 g Sugar: 4 g Fiber: 6 g Fat: 10 g Satu- rated Fat: 5 g Protein: 10 g Sodium: 426 mg

MAPLE LEMON TEMPEH CUBES

COOKING: 30-40' PREPARATION: 10' SERVES: 4

INGREDIENTS
- Tempeh; 1 packet
- Coconut oil; 2 to 3 teaspoons
- Lemon juice; 3 tablespoons
- Maple syrup; 2 teaspoons
- Bragg's Liquid Aminos or low-sodium tamari or (optional); 1 to 2 teaspoons
- Water; 2 teaspoons
- Dried basil; 1/4 teaspoon
- Powdered garlic; 1/4 teaspoon
- Black pepper (freshly grounded); to taste

DIRECTIONS
1. Heat your oven to 400 ° C.
2. Cut your tempeh block into squares in bite form.
3. Heat coconut oil over medium to high heat in a non- stick skillet.
4. When melted and heated, add the tempeh and cook on one side for 2-4 minutes, or until the tempeh turns down into a golden-brown color.
5. Flip the tempeh bits and cook for 2-4 minutes.
6. Mix the lemon juice, tamari, maple syrup, basil, water, garlic, and black pepper while tempeh is browning.
7. Drop the mixture over tempeh, then swirl to cover
the tempeh.
8. Sauté for 2-3 minutes, then turn the tempeh and sauté 1-2 minutes more.
9. The tempeh, on both sides, should be soft and orange.

NUTRITIONS: Carbohydrates: 22 Cal Fats: 17 g Sugar: 5 g Protein: 21 g Fiber: 9 g

SIMPLE BEEF ROAST

COOKING: 8H PREPARATION: 10' SERVES: 8

INGREDIENTS
- 5 pounds' beef roast
- 2 tablespoons Italian seasoning
- 1 cup beef stock
- 1 tablespoon sweet paprika
- 3 tablespoons olive oil

DIRECTIONS
1. In your slow cooker, mix all the ingredients, cover, and cook on low for 8 hours.
2. Carve the roast, divide it between plates and serve.

NUTRITIONS: Calories: 587 Fat: 24.1g Fiber: 0.3g Carbs: 0.9g Protein: 86.5g

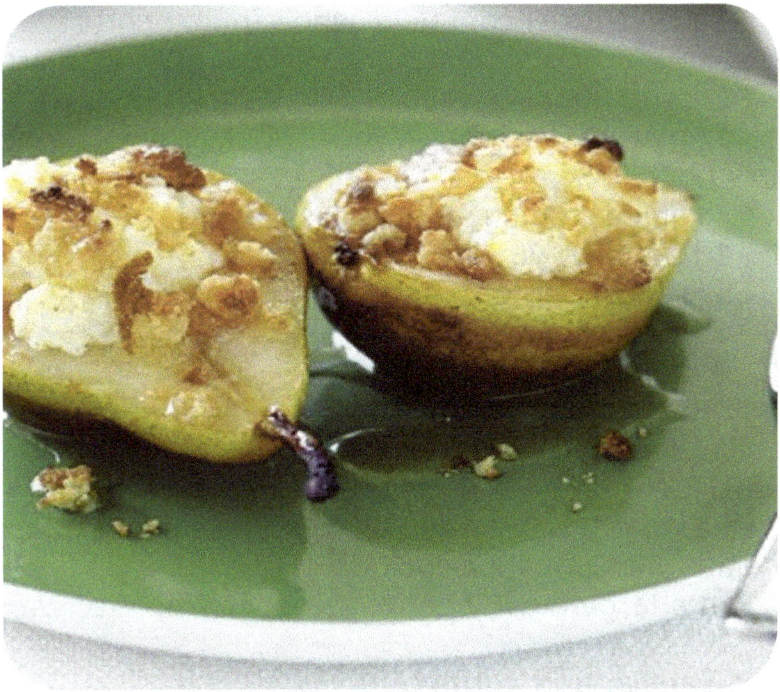

BAKED RICOTTA WITH PEARS

COOKING: 25' PREPARATION: 5' SERVES: 4

INGREDIENTS
- Nonstick cooking spray
- 1 (16-ounce) container whole-milk ricotta cheese
- 2 large eggs
- 1/4 cup white whole-wheat flour or whole-wheat pastry flour
- 1 tablespoon sugar
- 1 teaspoon vanilla extract
- 1/4 teaspoon ground nutmeg
- 1 pear, cored and diced
- 2 tablespoons water
- 1 tablespoon honey

DIRECTIONS
1. Preheat the oven to 400°F. Spray four 6-ounce ramekins with nonstick cooking spray.
2. In a large bowl, beat together the ricotta, eggs, flour, sugar, vanilla, and nutmeg.
3. Spoon into the ramekins.
4. Bake for 22 to 25 minutes, or until the ricotta is just about set.
5. Remove from the oven and cool slightly on racks.
6. While the ricotta is baking, in a small saucepan over medium heat, simmer the pear in the water for 10 minutes, until slightly softened.
7. Remove from the heat and stir in the honey.
8. Serve the ricotta ramekins topped with the warmed pear.

NUTRITIONS: Calories: 312 Cal Fat: 17g Cholesterol: 163mg Sodium: 130mg Carbohydrates: 23g Fiber: 2g Protein 17g

CHICKEN BREAST SOUP

COOKING: 4H PREPARATION: 5' SERVES: 4

INGREDIENTS
- 3 chicken breasts, skinless, boneless, cubed
- 2 celery stalks, chopped
- 2 carrots, chopped
- 2 tablespoons olive oil
- 1 red onion, chopped
- 3 garlic cloves, minced
- 4 cups chicken stock
- 1 tablespoon parsley, chopped

DIRECTIONS

1. In your slow cooker, mix all the ingredients except
the parsley, cover and cook on High for 4 hours.
2. Add the parsley, stir, ladle the soup into bowls and serve.

NUTRITIONS: Calories: 387 Fat: 21.1g Fiber: 8.93g Carbs: 26.3g Protein: 25.4g

MEDITERRANEAN BURRITO

COOKING: 0' PREPARATION: 10' SERVES: 2

INGREDIENTS
- 2 wheat tortillas
- 2 oz. red kidney beans, canned, drained
- 2 tablespoons hummus
- 2 teaspoons tahini sauce
- 1 cucumber
- 2 lettuce leaves
- 1 tablespoon lime juice
- 1 teaspoon olive oil
- ½ teaspoon dried oregano

DIRECTIONS
1. Mash the red kidney beans until you get a puree.
2. Then spread the wheat tortillas with beans mash from one side.
3. Add hummus and tahini sauce.
4. Cut the cucumber into the wedges and place them
over tahini sauce.
5. Then add lettuce leaves.
6. Make the dressing: mix up together olive oil, dried
oregano, and lime juice.
7. Drizzle the lettuce leaves with the dressing and wrap
the wheat tortillas in the shape of burritos.

NUTRITIONS: Calories: 288 Fat: 10.2 Fiber: 14.6 Carbs: 38.2 Protein: 12.5

CHICKEN SALAD WITH PINEAPPLE AND PECANS

COOKING: 5' PREPARATION: 10' SERVES: 4

INGREDIENTS

- (6-ounce) Boneless, skinless, cooked and cubed chicken breast
- Tablespoons of celery hacked
- Cut 1/4 cup of pineapple
- 1/4 cup orange peeled segments
- Tablespoon of pecans hacked
- 1/4 cup seedless grapes
- Salt and black chili pepper, to taste
- Cups cut from roman lettuce

DIRECTIONS

1. Put chicken, celery, pineapple, grapes, pecans, and raisins in a medium dish.
2. Kindly blend until mixed with a spoon, then season
with salt and pepper.
3. Create a bed of lettuce on a plate.
4. Cover with mixture of chicken and serve.

NUTRITIONS: Calories: 386 Cal Carbohydrates: 20 g Fat: 19 g Protein: 25 g

SNACKS RECIPES

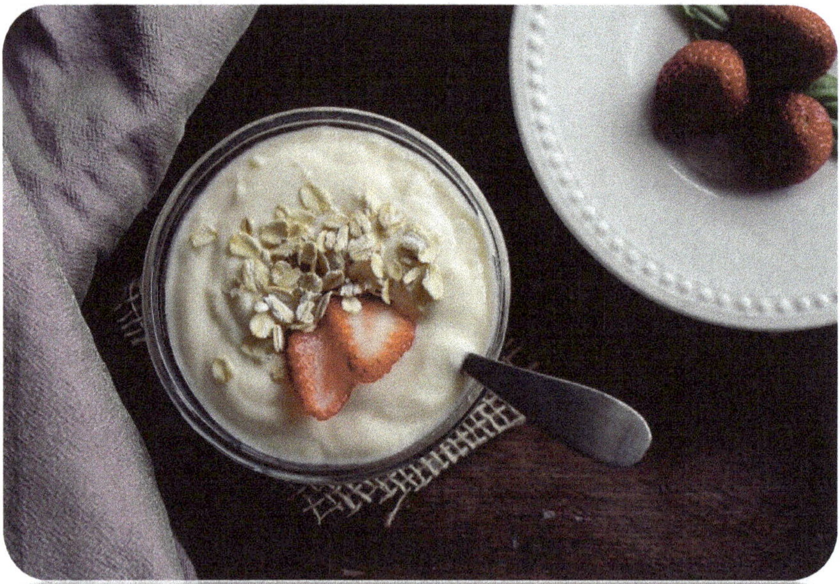

HUMMUS WITH GROUND LAMB

COOKING: 15' PREPARATION: 10'SERVES: 8

INGREDIENTS
- 10 ounces hummus
- 12 ounces lamb meat, ground
- ½ cup pomegranate seeds
- ¼ cup parsley, chopped
- 1 tablespoon olive oil
- Pita chips for serving

DIRECTIONS
1. Heat oil in a pan over medium-high heat, add the
meat, and brown for 15 minutes stirring often.
2. Spread the hummus on a platter, spread the ground lamb all over, also spread the pomegranate seeds and the parsley and serve with pita chips as a snack.

NUTRITIONS: Calories 133 Fat 9.7 g Fiber 1.7 g Carbs 6.4 g Protein 5 g

WRAPPED PLUMS

COOKING: 0' PREPARATION: 5' SERVES: 8

INGREDIENTS
- 2 ounces prosciutto, cut into 16 pieces
- 4 plums, quartered
- 1 tablespoon chives, chopped
- A pinch of red pepper flakes, crushed

DIRECTIONS
1. Wrap each plum quarter in a prosciutto slice, arrange them all on a platter, sprinkle the chives and pepper flakes all over and serve.

NUTRITIONS: Calories 30 Fat 1 g Fiber 0 g Carbs 4 g Protein 2 g

CHILI MANGO AND WATERMELON SALSA

COOKING: 0' PREPARATION: 5' SERVES: 12

INGREDIENTS
- 1 red tomato, chopped
- Salt and black pepper to the taste
- 1 cup watermelon, seedless, peeled and cubed
- 1 red onion, chopped
- 2 mangoes, peeled and chopped
- 2 chili peppers, chopped
- ¼ cup cilantro, chopped
- 3 tablespoons lime juice
- Pita chips for serving

DIRECTIONS

1. In a bowl, mix the tomato with the watermelon, the onion and the rest of the ingredients except the pita chips and toss well. Divide the mix into small cups and serve with pita chips on the side.

NUTRITIONS: Calories 62 Fat g Fiber 1.3 g Carbs 3.9 g Protein 2.3 g

CREAMY SPINACH AND SHALLOTS DIP

COOKING: 0' PREPARATION: 10 'SERVES: 4

INGREDIENTS
- 1 pound spinach, roughly chopped
- 2 shallots, chopped
- 2 tablespoons mint, chopped
- ¾ cup cream cheese, soft
- Salt and black pepper to the taste

DIRECTIONS

1. Combine the spinach with the shallots and the rest of the ingredients in a blender, and pulse well. Divide into small bowls and serve as a party dip.

NUTRITIONS: Calories 204 Fat 11.5 g Fiber 3.1 g Carbs 4.2 g Protein 5.9 g

GOAT CHEESE AND CHIVES SPREAD

COOKING: 0' PREPARATION: 10'SERVES: 4

INGREDIENTS
- 2 ounces goat cheese, crumbled
- ¾ cup sour cream
- 2 tablespoons chives, chopped
- 1 tablespoon lemon juice
- Salt and black pepper to the taste
- 2 tablespoons extra virgin olive oil

DIRECTIONS

1. Mix the goat cheese with the cream and the rest of the ingredients in a bowl, and whisk really well. Keep in the fridge for 10 minutes and serve as a party spread.

NUTRITIONS: Calories 220 Fat 11.5 g Fiber 4.8 g Carbs 8.9 g Protein 5.6 g

MEDITERRANEAN CHICKEN SALAD

COOKING: 30' PREPARATION: 15'SERVES: 4

INGREDIENTS
- For Chicken:
- 1 3/4 lb. boneless, skinless chicken breast
- 1/4 teaspoon each of pepper and salt (or as desired)
- 1 1/2 tablespoon of butter, melted
- For Mediterranean Salad:
- 1 cup of sliced cucumber
- 6 cups of romaine lettuce, that is torn or roughly chopped
- 10 pitted Kalamata olives
- 1 pint of cherry tomatoes
- 1/3 cup of reduced-fat feta cheese
- 1/4 teaspoon each of pepper and salt (or lesser)
- 1 small lemon juice (it should be about 2 tablespoons)

DIRECTIONS

1. Preheat your oven or grill to about 3500F.
2. Season the chicken with salt, butter, and black pep- per
3. Roast or grill chicken until it reaches an internal temperature of 1650F in about 25 minutes.
4. Once your chicken breasts are cooked, remove and keep aside to rest for about 5 minutes before you slice
5. it.
6. Combine all the salad ingredients you have and toss
everything together very well
7. Serve the chicken with Mediterranean salad

NUTRITIONS: Calories: 340 Cal Protein: 45 g Carbohydrates: 9 g Fat: 14 g

LAMB STUFFED AVOCADO

COOKING: 40' PREPARATION: 10' SERVES: 4

INGREDIENTS
- 2 avocados
- 1 1/2 cup minced lamb
- 1/2 cup cheddar cheese, grated
- 1/2 cup parmesan cheese, grated
- 2 tbsp almond, chopped
- 1 tbsp coriander, chopped
- 2 tbsp olive oil
- 1 tomato, chopped
- 1 jalapeno, chopped
- Salt and pepper to taste
- 1 tsp. garlic, chopped
- 1 inch ginger, chopped

DIRECTIONS
1. Cut the avocados in half. Remove the pit and scoop out some flesh to stuff it later.
2. In a skillet, add half of the oil.
3. Toss the ginger, garlic for 1 minute.
4. Add the lamb and toss for 3 minutes.
5. Add the tomato, coriander, parmesan, jalapeno, salt, pepper, and cook for 2 minutes.
6. Take off the heat. Stuff the avocados.
7. Sprinkle the almonds, cheddar cheese, and add olive oil on top.
8. Add to a baking sheet and bake for 30 minutes. Serve.

NUTRITIONS: Fat: 19.5 g Cholesterol: 167.5 mg
Sodium: 410.7 mg Potassium: 617.1 mg
Carbohydrate: 13.1 g

VEGETABLES

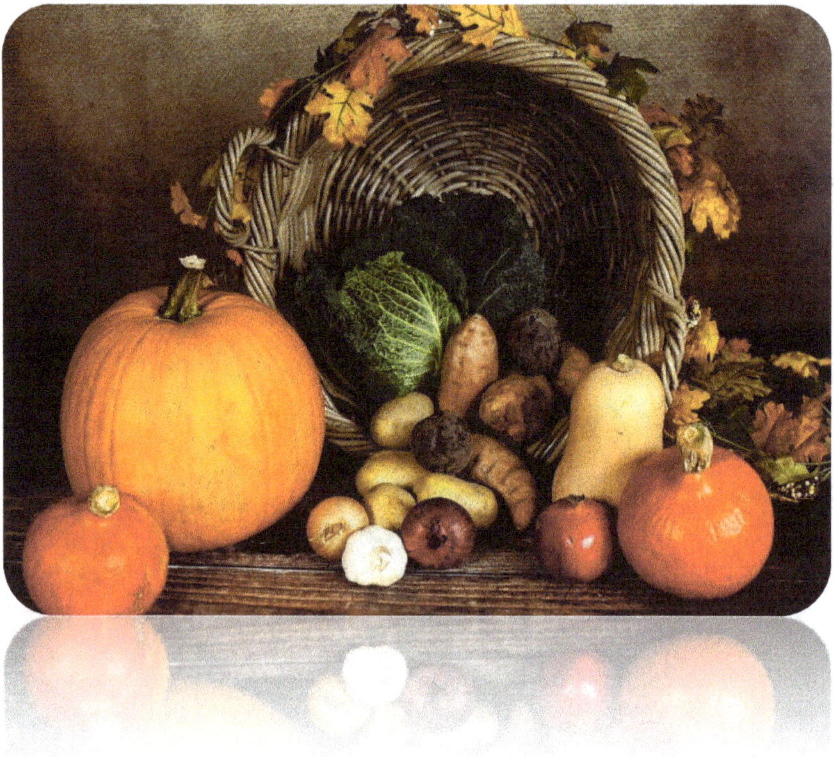

ASPARAGUS GREEN SCRAMBLE

COOKING: 6' INGREDIENTS

PREPARATION: 5'
DIRECTIONS

SERVES: 2

- » 3 eggs
- » 1 Portobello mushroom, chopped
- » 2 garlic cloves, chopped
- » 1/2 cup spinach
- » 4 asparagus, trimmed, diced
- » Sea salt to taste
- » Cayenne pepper to taste
- » 1 tbsp olive oil

1. In a bowl, whisk the eggs with salt and cayenne pepper.
2. In a skillet, add the oil and pour in the egg mix.
3. Cook for 1 minute.
4. Add the spinach, mushroom, asparagus, and garlic.
5. Stir for 4 minutes. Serve.

NUTRITIONS: Carbohydrates: 3 g Fat: 6 g Protein: 13 g

HEALTHY BROCCOLI SALAD

COOKING: 25' PREPARATION: 5'SERVES: 6

INGREDIENTS
- 3 cups broccoli, chopped
- 1 tbsp apple cider vinegar
- 1/2 cup Greek yogurt
- 2 tbsp sunflower seeds
- 3 bacon slices, cooked and chopped
- 1/3 cup onion, sliced
- 1/4 tsp. stevia

DIRECTIONS
1. In a mixing bowl, mix broccoli, onion, and bacon.
2. In a small bowl, mix yogurt, vinegar, and stevia and pour over broccoli mixture.
3. Stir to combine.
4. Sprinkle sunflower seeds on top of the salad.
5. Store salad in the refrigerator for 30 minutes.
6. Serve and enjoy.

NUTRITIONS: Calories: 90 Cal Fat: 4.9 g Carbohydrates: 5.4 g Sugar: 2.5 g Protein: 6.2 g Cholesterol: 12 mg

CRISPY RYE BREAD SNACKS WITH GUACAMOLE AND ANCHOVIES

COOKING: 10'   PREPARATION: 10'   SERVES: 4

INGREDIENTS
» 4 slices of rye bread
» Guacamole
» Anchovies in oil

DIRECTIONS
1. Cut each slice of bread into 3 strips of bread.
2. Place in the basket of the air fryer, without piling up, and we go in batches giving it the touch you want to give it. You can select 1800C, 10 minutes.
3. When you have all the crusty rye bread strips, put a layer of guacamole on top, whether homemade or commercial.
4. In each bread, place 2 anchovies on the guacamole.

NUTRITIONS: Calories: 180 Carbs: 4 g Fat: 11 g Protein: 4 g Fiber: 09 g

MUSHROOMS STUFFED WITH TOMATO

COOKING: 50' PREPARATION: 5' SERVES: 4

INGREDIENTS

- 8 large mushrooms
- 250g of minced meat
- 4 cloves of garlic
- Extra virgin olive oil
- Salt
- Ground pepper
- Flour, beaten egg and breadcrumbs
- Frying oil
- Fried Tomato Sauce

DIRECTIONS

1. Remove the stem from the mushrooms and chop it. Peel the garlic and chop. Put some extra virgin olive oil in a pan and add the garlic and mushroom stems.
2. Sauté and add the minced meat. Sauté well until the
meat is well cooked and season.
3. Fill the mushrooms with the minced meat.
4. Press well and take the freezer for 30 minutes.
5. Pass the mushrooms with flour, beaten egg and breadcrumbs. Beaten egg and breadcrumbs.
6. Place the mushrooms in the basket of the air fryer.
7. Select 20 minutes, 1800C.
8. Distribute the mushrooms once cooked in the dishes.

9. Heat the tomato sauce and cover the stuffed mush- rooms.

NUTRITIONS: Calories: 160 Carbs: 2 g Fat: 11 g Protein: 4 g

KALE SLAW AND STRAWBERRY SALAD + POPPYSEED DRESSING

COOKING: 20' PREPARATION: 10' SERVES: 2

INGREDIENTS

- Chicken breast; 8 ounces; sliced and baked
- Kale; 1 cup; chopped
- Slaw mix; 1 cup (cabbage, broccoli slaw, carrots mixed)
- Slivered almonds; 1/4 cup
- Strawberries; 1 cup; sliced
- For the dressing:
- Light mayonnaise; 1 tablespoon
- Dijon mustard
- Olive oil; 1 tablespoon
- Apple cider vinegar; 1 tablespoon
- Lemon juice; 1/2 teaspoon
- 1 tablespoon of Honey
- Onion powder; 1/4 teaspoon
- Garlic powder; 1/4 teaspoon
- Poppyseeds

DIRECTIONS

1. Whisk the dressing ingredients together until well mixed, then leave to cool in the fridge.
2. Slice the chicken breasts.
3. Divide 2 bowls of spinach, slaw, and strawberries.
4. Cover with a sliced breast of chicken (4 oz. each),

then scatter with almonds.
5.   Divide the salad over the dressing and drizzle.

NUTRITIONS: Calories: 340 Cal Fats: 13.6 g Saturated Fat: 6.2 g

ROASTED ROOT VEGETABLES

COOKING: 6-8 H PREPARATION: 20' SERVES: 8

INGREDIENTS

- » 6 carrots, cut into 1-inch chunks
- » 2 yellow onions, each cut into 8 wedges
- » 2 sweet potatoes, peeled and cut into chunks
- » 6 Yukon Gold potatoes, cut into chunks
- » 8 whole garlic cloves, peeled
- » 4 parsnips, peeled and cut into chunks
- » 3 tablespoons olive oil
- » 1 teaspoon dried thyme leaves
- » 1/2 teaspoon salt
- » 1/8 teaspoon freshly ground black pepper

DIRECTIONS
1. In a 6-quart slow cooker, mix all of the ingredients.
2. Cover and cook on low for 6 to 8 hours, or until the vegetables are tender.

NUTRITIONS: Calories: 214 Cal Carbohydrates: 40 g Sugar: 7 g Fiber: 6 g Fat: 5 g Saturated Fat: 1 g Protein: 4 g Sodium: 201 mg

GRILLED EGGPLANTS

COOKING: 10' PREPARATION: 10' SERVES: 4

INGREDIENTS

- 1 large eggplant, cut into thick circles
- Salt and pepper to taste
- 1 tsp. smoked paprika
- 1 tbsp coconut flour
- 1 tsp. lime juice
- 1 tbsp olive oil

DIRECTIONS

1. Coat the eggplants in smoked paprika, salt, pepper, lime juice, coconut flour, and let it sit for 10 minutes.
2. In a grilling pan, add the olive oil.
3. Grill the eggplants for 3 minutes on each side.
4. Serve.

NUTRITIONS: Fat: 0.1 g Sodium: 1.6 mg Carbohydrates: 4.8 g Fiber: 2.4 g Sugars: 2.9 g Protein: 0.8 g

MEAT

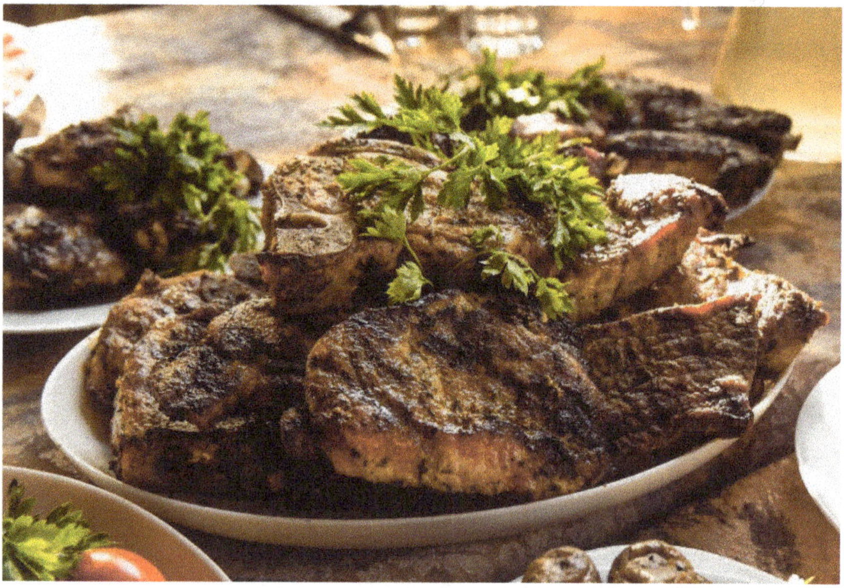

TURKEY TACO

COOKING: 20' PREPARATION: 10' SERVES: 4

INGREDIENTS

- 2 pre-made rolls (1/3 lean, 1 1/3 condiment)
- 4 ounces of turkey (2/3 thin) white meat leftover from Thanksgiving!
- 2 Tablespoons of salad with cranberry (1/4 snack, 1/8th green)
- Shredded laitoux

DIRECTIONS

1. Toast the buns with 2.
2. Next put 1 tablespoon of sugar-free cranberry salad, then 2 ounces of turkey and top with a little shredded lettuce.
3. Fold up like a taco, and eat. 2 Tacos is equivalent to 1 serving.
4. 1 Lean, 1/3 seasoning, 1/4 snack, 1/8 orange.
5. You will need to combine this with a green to make it a lean and nutritious meal in its entirety.

NUTRITIONS: Protein: 17.6 g Carbohydrates: 4.8 g Fats: 7.2 g Cholesterol: 62.7 mg

BRAISED COLLARD GREENS IN PEANUT SAUCE WITH PORK TENDERLOIN

COOKING: 60'   PREPARATION: 10'   SERVES: 4

INGREDIENTS
- 2 cups of chicken stock
- 12 cups of chopped collard greens
- 5 tablespoon of powdered peanut butter
- 3 cloves of garlic, crushed
- 1 teaspoon of salt
- 1/2 teaspoon of allspice
- 1/2 teaspoon of black pepper
- 2 teaspoon of lemon juice
- 3/4 teaspoon of hot sauce
- 1 1/2 lb. of pork tenderloin

DIRECTIONS
1. Get a pot with a tight-fitting lid and combine the collards with the garlic, chicken stock, hot sauce, and half of the pepper and salt.
2. Cook on low heat for about 1 hour or until the col- lards become tender.
3. Once the collards are tender, stir in the allspice, lemon juice.
4. And powdered peanut butter.
5. Keep warm.
6. Season the pork tenderloin with the remaining pepper and salt, and broil in a toaster oven for 10 minutes when you have an internal temperature of 1450F.
7. Make sure to turn the tenderloin every 2 minutes to
achieve an even browning all over.

8. After that, you can take away the pork from the oven and allow it to rest for like 5 minutes.
9. Slice the pork as you will like and serve it on top of
the braised greens.

NUTRITIONS: Calories: 320 Cal Fat: 10 g
Carbohydrates: 15 g Protein: 45 g

CHICKEN CRUST MARGHERITA PIZZA

COOKING: 30' PREPARATION: 15'SERVES: 2

INGREDIENTS
- 1/2 lb. ground chicken breast
- 1 egg
- 2 Tbsp grated parmesan cheese
- 1/2 tsp. Italian seasoning
- Cooking spray
- 1/2 cup no-sugar-added tomato sauce
- 1/2 cup reduced-fat shredded mozzarella cheese
- 2 plum tomatoes, sliced
- 1/4 cup chopped basil

DIRECTIONS
1. Preheat oven to 400 °F.
2. Arrange the first 4 ingredients in a medium-sized bowl.
3. Form the chicken mixture into a circular crust shape onto a parchment-lined, lightly greased baking sheet. Bake until golden, about 20 minutes.
4. Add cheese, sauce and tomato slice, and cook till cheese is melted about 10 minutes.
5. Finally, add fresh basil before serving.
6. After that, you can take away the pork from the oven and allow it to rest for like 5 minutes.
7. Slice the pork as you will like and serve it on top of the braised greens.

NUTRITIONS: Carbohydrates: 0.49 g Fats: 4.61 g
Cholesterol: 33 mg Sodium: 138 mg Protein: 11.14 g

TOMATO STEAK

COOKING: 25m PREPARATION: 10m SERVES: 2

INGREDIENTS

- 2 Sirloin steaks
- 1 garlic clove
- 250g tomato sauce
- 1 teaspoon oregano
- 3 spoon olive oil
- 2 tablespoons of white flour
- 1 mozzarella
- Salt and pepper to taste

DIRECTIONS

Oil and flour the two steaks.
Chop the garlic clove and sigh it with the olive oil.
Add the steaks and let them simmer in the pan for 10 minutes.
Add the tomato and oregano and cook for another 10 minutes by raising the heat.
Taste and correct salt and pepper.
100 seconds before removing them from the heat add a mozzarella cut into pieces.
Let the mozzarella melt the and serve!

NUTRITIONS:
Calories: 340 Cal Fats: 9 g Carbohydrates: 12g
Protein: 32g

TURKEY MEATBALLS

COOKING: 30m PREPARATION: 5m SERVES: 2

INGREDIENTS

- ½ Kilo minced turkey
- 1 eggs
- 2 spoons chopped coriander
- 1 spoon olive oil
- thyme to taste
- 100g breadcrumbs (Optional)
- 2 garlic clove
- Salt and pepper to taste

DIRECTIONS

Mix all the ingredient well and form some little balls. Put in the oven for 30 minutes at 200 degrees. Ready to serve and enjoy!

NUTRITIONS:
Calories: 320 Cal Fats: 7 g Carbohydrates: 11g Protein: 30g

ALMOND CUTLETS

COOKING: 30 PREPARATION: 5m SERVES: 2

INGREDIENTS

- 1 chicken breast
- 2 eggs
- 5 spoon olive oil
- 500g breadcrumbs
- 200g almond flour
- 1 garlic clove
- 2 spoon of grated parmesan cheese
- 1 spoon chopped coriander to taste
- Salt and pepper to taste

DIRECTIONS

Cut the chicken breast into 4 slices.
Oil and sprinkle with almond flour.
Set them aside and prepare the necessary to bread the slices of chicken.
Break the eggs into a bowl and beat them with a fork.
Separately prepare a flat dish with the crumb topped with the garlic clove chopped coriander, parmesan, salt and black pepper.
Take the smattered chicken slices with the almond, first pass them into the egg and then into the flour to form a second breading.
Put them in the oven for about half an hour.
Ready to be enjoyed with a green salad!

NUTRITIONS:
Calories: 290 Cal Fats: 8 g Carbohydrates: 13g
Protein: 32g

PORK SHANK WITH POTATO

COOKING: 1 ,1/2 h PREPARATION: 10m SERVES: 4

INGREDIENTS

- 1 pork shin of about 1 kg
- 1/2 kg potatoes
- Veg mix (1 celery stem, 1 whole garlic clove, 1 carrot and an onion)
- 5 tablespoon olive oil
- Mixed of your favourite spices (juniper, sage, rosemary, thyme)
- Vegetable broth 100 ml
- 1 glass of white wine
- Some bay leaf
- Salt and pepper to taste

DIRECTIONS

Get a thick-bottomed pan and sauté the mixture of chopped vegetables with 2 tablespoons of olive oil add the shank and sauté well turning it every 5 minutes for 20 minutes.
Add the wine, bay leaves and spice mixture and cook for another 10 minutes turning the shank back.
Add the vegetable broth and cook for another 10 minutes in the pan. Meanwhile in a large baking tray put the cut potatoes of the shape you prefer and cook them at 200 degrees for 20 minutes.
Transfer the contents of the pan to the baking tray above the potatoes and cook for 60 minutes at 170 degrees.

NUTRITIONS:
Calories: 350 Fats: 14 g Carbohydrates: 13g Protein: 25

SOUPS AND STEWS

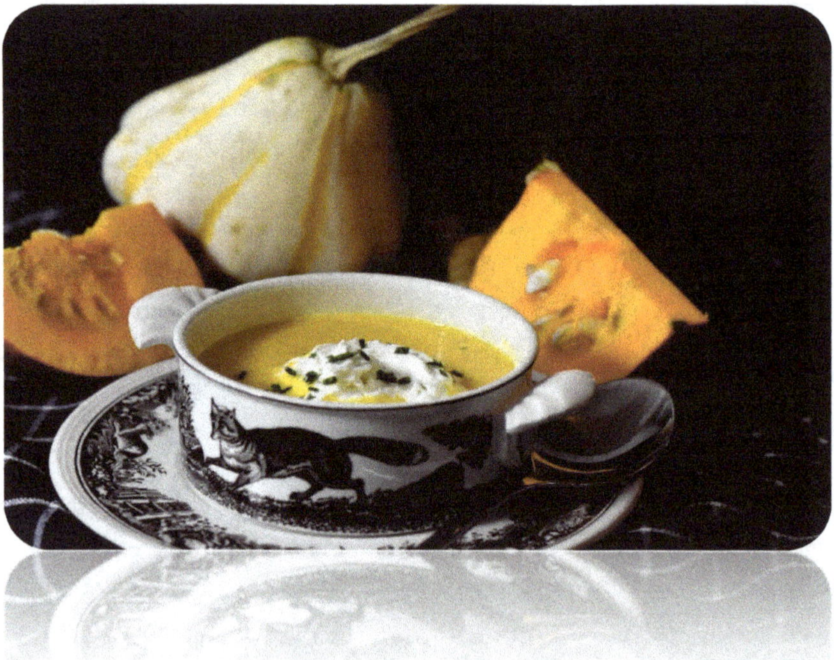

TOFU STIR FRY WITH ASPARAGUS

COOKING: 30' PREPARATION: 15'SERVES: 4

INGREDIENTS
- 1 pound asparagus, cut off stems
- 2 tbsp olive oil
- 2 blocks tofu, pressed and cubed
- 2 garlic cloves, minced
- 1 tsp. cajun spice mix
- 1 tsp. mustard
- 1 bell pepper, chopped
- 1/4 cup vegetable broth
- Salt and black pepper, to taste

DIRECTIONS
1. In a large saucepan with lightly salted water, place in asparagus and cook until tender for 10 minutes; drain.
2. Set a wok over high heat and warm olive oil; stir in tofu cubes and cook for 6 minutes.
3. Place in garlic and cook for 30 seconds until soft.
4. Stir in the rest of the ingredients, including reserved
asparagus, and cook for an additional 4 minutes.
5. Divide among plates and serve.

NUTRITIONS: Calories: 138 Fat: 8.9 g Carbohydrates: 5.9 g Protein: 6.4 g

CREAM OF THYME TOMATO SOUP

COOKING: 20' PREPARATION: 5' SERVES: 6

INGREDIENTS

- 2 tbsp ghee
- 2 large red onions, diced
- 1/2 cup raw cashew nuts, diced
- 2 (28 oz.) cans tomatoes
- 1 tsp. fresh thyme leaves + extra to garnish
- 1 1/2 cups water
- Salt and black pepper to taste

DIRECTIONS

1. Melt ghee in a pot over medium heat and sauté the onions for 4 minutes until softened.
2. Stir in the tomatoes, thyme, water, cashews, and season with salt and black pepper.
3. Cover and bring to simmer for 10 minutes until thoroughly cooked.
4. Open, turn the heat off, and puree the ingredients with an immersion blender.
5. Adjust to taste and stir in the heavy cream.
6. Spoon into soup bowls and serve.

NUTRITIONS: Calories: 310 Cal Fats: 27 g Carbohydrates: 3g Protein: 11g

SAVORY SPLIT PEA SOUP

PREPARATION: 5' SERVES: 6

INGREDIENTS

- » 1 (16-ounce) package dried green split peas, soaked overnight
- » 5 cups vegetable broth or water
- » 2 teaspoons garlic powder
- » 2 teaspoons onion powder
- » 1 teaspoon dried oregano
- » 1 teaspoon dried thyme
- » 1/4 teaspoon freshly ground black pepper
- »

DIRECTIONS

1. In a large stockpot, combine the split peas, broth, garlic powder, onion powder, oregano, thyme, and pepper.
2. Bring to a boil over medium-high heat.
3. Cover, reduce the heat to medium-low, and simmer for 45 minutes, stirring every 5 to 10 minutes. Serve warm.

NUTRITIONS: Fat: 2 g Carbohydrates: 48 g Fiber: 20 g Protein: 23 g

EASY FISH SOUP

COOKING: 40m PREPARATION: 10m SERVES: 4

INGREDIENTS

- 8 king prawns
- 2 cod fillets
- 2 toad tail fillets
- 2 Monkfish fillets
- 3 tablespoons extra virgin olive oil
- 2 cloves garlic
- 1 carrot
- 1 onion
- 2 spoons of chopped parsley
- 1 glass of white wine
- Salt and pepper to taste
- 200ml tomato sauce
- 400 ml homemade Fish broth

DIRECTIONS
Make sure fish fillets are spine-free and cut into thin pieces.
In a pot sauté the chopped vegetables with olive oil, add the fish, the white wine and cook for 10 minutes.
Add the tomato sauce and fish broth and cook for other 30 minutes.
Taste and correct salt and black pepper.

NUTRITIONS:
Calories: 260 Fats: 4 g Carbohydrates: 6g Protein: 29g

HOME MADE FISH BROTH

COOKING: 30m PREPARATION: 10m SERVES: /

INGREDIENTS

- 1 white onion
- 1 celery stick
- 1 carrot
- 2 tablespoons olive oil
- 1 tablespoon chopped parsley
- Molluscs such as mussels or clams
- Fish heads and bones that you eliminate after obtaining the net meat fillet
- 2 l of water
- 1 tablespoon salt

DIRECTIONS

Roughly chop the vegetables and sauté them with olive oil, add the fish offal and shellfish, cover everything with water and boil for half an hour.
Set aside and let cool. If you can keep all night in the fridge to release as much flavour as possible from the fish.
Strain carefully and store in the fridge.

NUTRITIONS:
Calories: 60 Fats: 0.2g Carbohydrates: 0.9g Protein: 2g

ROMANIAN BEEF SOUP

COOKING: 70m PREPARATION: 10m SERVES: 2

INGREDIENTS

- 1 litre of homemade beef broth
- 2 steaks of 200g each
- 1 onion
- Some bay leaf
- 10 dry porcini mushrooms
- 1 tablespoon parsley
- 3 tablespoons olive oil
- 1 spoon of parmesan cheese
- Salt and pepper to taste

DIRECTIONS

Chop the onion finely and sauté with olive oil, add the bay leaves and dried porcini.
Sauté for 5 minutes then add the meat cut into squares with a knife.
Add the broth and cook for 1 hour.
Taste and add the salt and black pepper.
Serve with chopped parsley and grated Parmesan cheese.

NUTRITIONS:
Calories: 270 Fats: 4.2g Carbohydrates: 3.7g Protein: 18g

HOMEMADE BEEF BROTH

COOKING: 2h PREPARATION: 10m SERVES: 2

INGREDIENTS

- 1 Piece of meat(about half a kilo)
- Beef bones
- 2 celery sticks
- 2 carrots
- 2 onions
- 6 ripe wine tomatoes
- 3 litres of water
- 4 tablespoons olive oil
- Spice mixture (Cloves, whole black pepper, rosemary)
- Salt to taste

DIRECTIONS

Put all the ingredients in a pan and let it cook for 2 hours.
Put aside and let it chill the whole night.
Strain and store in the fridge.

NUTRITIONS:
Calories: 90 Fats: 1.4g Carbohydrates: 1.5g Protein: 7g

ALL GREEN SOUPS

COOKING: 40m PREPARATION: 10m SERVES: 4

INGREDINETS

- 200g kale
- 1 head of broccoli
- 2 zucchini
- 200g peas
- 2 celery sticks
- 1 clove of garlic
- 2 spoon olive oil
- 2 litre of water
- 1 vegetables stock cube
- Parmesan cheese to taste (Optional)
- Salt to taste

DIRECTIONS
Chop the clove of garlic, sauté it with olive oil.
Add the vegetables a little at a time.
Add 2 litres of water.
Boil and lower the flame.
Cook with the low flame for another 40 minutes.
Insert the cube veg stock and turn until it melts.
Taste and correct salt if necessary.
Serve with a sprinkle of parmesan.

NUTRITIONS:
Calories: 220 Fats: 2.6g Carbohydrates: 3.5g Protein: 13g

SMOOTHIES

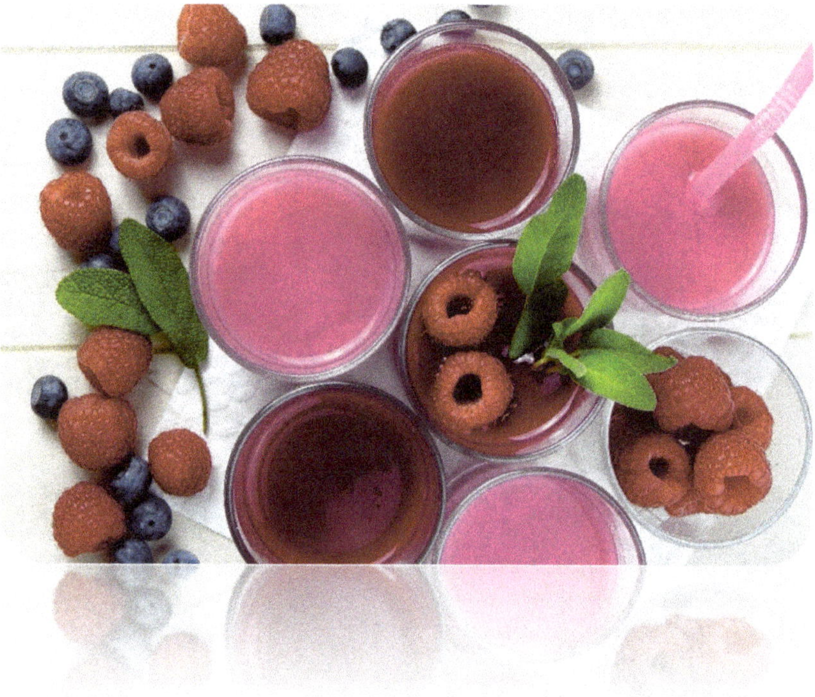

AVOCADO BLUEBERRY SMOOTHIE

COOKING: 5' PREPARATION: 5'SERVES: 1

INGREDIENTS

- 1 tsp chia seeds
- ½ cup unsweetened coconut milk
- 1 avocado
- ½ cup blueberries

DIRECTIONS

1. Add all the listed ingredients to the blender and blend until smooth and creamy.
2. Serve immediately and enjoy.

NUTRITIONS: Calories: 389 Fat: 34.6g Carbs: 20.7g Protein: 4.8g Fiber: 0g

VEGAN BLUEBERRY SMOOTHIE

COOKING: 5' PREPARATION: 5'SERVES: 2

INGREDIENTS

- 2 cups blueberries
- 1 tbsp hemp seeds
- 1 tbsp chia seeds
- 1 tbsp flax meal
- 1/8 tsp orange zest, grated
- 1 cup fresh orange juice
- 1 cup unsweetened coconut milk

DIRECTIONS

1. Toss all your ingredients into your blender then process till smooth and creamy.
2. Serve immediately and enjoy.

NUTRITIONS: Calories: 212 Fat: 6.6g Carbs: 36.9g Protein: 5.2g Fiber: 0g

REFRESHING CUCUMBER SMOOTHIE

COOKING: 5' PREPARATION: 5'SERVES: 2

INGREDIENTS

- 1 cup ice cubes
- 20 drops liquid stevia
- 2 fresh lime, peeled and halved
- 1 tsp lime zest, grated
- 1 cucumber, chopped
- 1 avocado, pitted and peeled
- 2 cups kale
- 1 tbsp creamed coconut
- ¾ cup coconut water

DIRECTIONS

1. Toss all your ingredients into your blender then process till smooth and creamy.
2. Serve immediately and enjoy.

NUTRITIONS: Calories: 313 Fat: 25.1g Carbs: 24.7g Protein: 4.9g Fiber: 0g

CAULIFLOWER VEGGIE SMOOTHIE

COOKING: 5' PREPARATION: 5'SERVES: 2

INGREDIENTS

- 1 zucchini, peeled and chopped
- 1 Seville orange, peeled
- 1 apple, diced
- 1 banana
- 1 cup kale
- ½ cup cauliflower

DIRECTIONS

1. Toss all your ingredients into your blender then process till smooth and creamy.
2. Serve immediately and enjoy.

NUTRITIONS: Calories: 71 Fat: 0.3g Carbs: 18.3g Protein: 1.3g Fiber: 0g

PRICKLY PEAR JUICE

COOKING: 10' PREPARATION: 5' SERVES: 2

INGREDIENTS

- » 6 Prickly Pears
- » 1/3 cup of Lime Juice
- » 1/3 cup of Agave
- » 1-1/2 cups of Spring Water*

DIRECTIONS

1. Take Prickly Pear, cut off the ends, slice off the skin, and put in a blender. Do the same with the other pears.
2. Add Lime Juice with Agave to the blender and blend
well for 30–40 seconds.
3. Strain the prepared mixture through a nut milk bag
or cheesecloth and pour it back into the blender.
4. Pour Spring Water in and blend it repeatedly.
5. Serve and enjoy your Prickly Pear Juice!
6. Useful Tips:
7. If you want a cold drink, add a tray of ice cubes instead.
8. like and serve it on top of the braised greens.

NUTRITIONS: Calories: 312 Fat: 6g Carbs: 11g Protein: 8g Fiber: 2g

PROTEIC LIQUID CHOCOLATE

COOKING: / PREPARATION: 3m SERVES: 2

INGREDINETS

- 80g peanut butter
- 2 dates
- 2 spoons cocoa powder
- 380 ml oat milk

DIRECTIONS

1. Toss all your ingredients into your blender then process till smooth and creamy.
2. Serve immediately and enjoy.

NUTRITIONS:
Calories: 270 Fats: 2.1g Carbohydrates: 4.5g Protein: 14g

BANANA YUMMY

COOKING: / PREPARATION: 3m SERVES: 1

INGREDINETS

- 40g peanut butter
- ½ banana
- 2 drops vanilla extract
- 180ml soia milk

DIRECTIONS

1. Toss all your ingredients into your blender then process till smooth and creamy.
2. Serve immediately and enjoy.

NUTRITIONS:
Calories: 220 Fats: 1.1g Carbohydrates: 2g Protein: 10g

EXOTIC PASSION

COOKING: / PREPARATION: 3m SERVES: 2

INGREDINETS

- 4 passion fruit
- ½ mango
- ½ papaya
- 300 ml Pineapple Juice

DIRECTIONS

1. Toss all your ingredients into your blender then process till smooth and creamy.
2. Serve immediately and enjoy.

NUTRITIONS:
Calories: 290 Fats: 4.1g Carbohydrates: 5g Protein: 2

DESSERTS

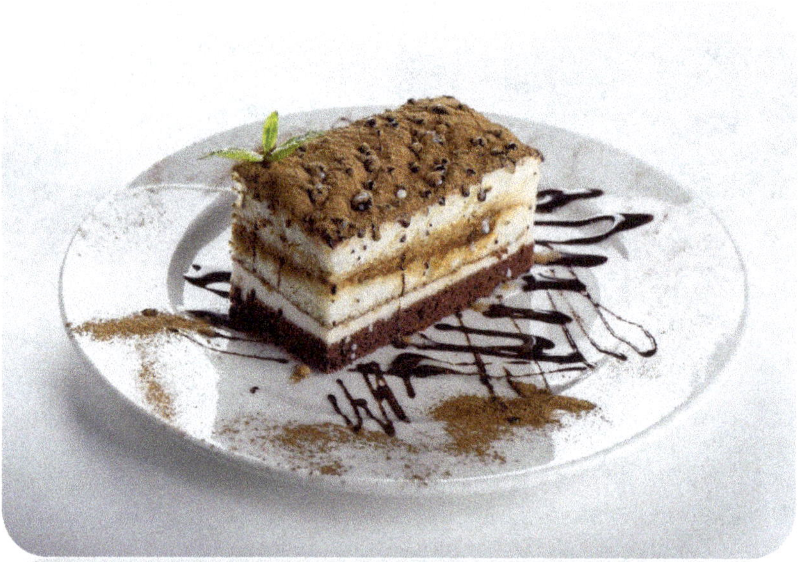

NO BAKE FUELING PEANUT BUTTER BROWNIES

COOKING: 30'   PREPARATION: 5' SERVES: 6

INGREDIENTS

- » 3 tablespoons peanut butter
- » 1 cup water
- » 6 packets Double Chocolate Brownie Fueling

DIRECTIONS
1. Put all ingredients in a bowl and mix until all elements are well incorporated.
2. Pour into silicone molds and place in the freezer.
3. Freeze for 30 minutes before eating.

NUTRITIONS: Calories per serving: 906 Cal Protein: 8.7 g Carbohydrates: 157 g Fat: 31.8 g

CHOCOLATE BARS

COOKING: 20' PREPARATION: 10'SERVES: 16

INGREDIENTS

- 15 oz cream cheese, softened
- 15 oz unsweetened dark chocolate
- 1 tsp vanilla
- 10 drops liquid stevia

DIRECTIONS

1. Grease 8-inch square dish and set aside.
2. In a saucepan dissolve chocolate over low heat.
3. Add stevia and vanilla and stir well.
4. Remove pan from heat and set aside.
5. Add cream cheese into the blender and blend until smooth.
6. Add melted chocolate mixture into the cream cheese
and blend until just combined.
7. Transfer mixture into the prepared dish and spread evenly and place in the refrigerator until firm.
8. Slice and serve.

NUTRITIONS: Calories: 230 Fat: 24 g Carbs: 7.5 g Sugar: 0.1 g Protein: 6 g Cholesterol: 29 mg

BLUEBERRY MUFFINS

COOKING: 35' PREPARATION: 15'SERVES: 12

INGREDIENTS

- 2 eggs
- 1/2 cup fresh blueberries
- 1 cup heavy cream
- 2 cups almond flour
- 1/4 tsp lemon zest
- 1/2 tsp lemon extract
- 1 tsp baking powder
- 5 drops stevia
- 1/4 cup butter, melted

DIRECTIONS

1. heat the cooker to 350 F. Line muffin tin with cup- cake liners and set aside.
2. Add eggs into the bowl and whisk until mix.
3. Add remaining ingredients and mix to combine.
4. Pour mixture into the prepared muffin tin and bake
for 25 minutes.
5. Serve and enjoy.

NUTRITIONS: Calories: 190 Fat: 17 g Carbs: 5 g Sugar: 1 g Protein: 5 g Cholesterol: 55

CHOCOLATE POPSICLE

COOKING: 10' PREPARATION: 20' SERVES: 6

INGREDIENTS

- 4 oz unsweetened chocolate, chopped
- 6 drops liquid stevia
- 1 1/2 cups heavy cream

DIRECTIONS

1. Add heavy cream into the microwave-safe bowl and microwave until just begins the boiling.
2. Add chocolate into the heavy cream and set aside for 5 minutes.
3. Add liquid stevia into the heavy cream mixture and
stir until chocolate is melted.
4. Pour mixture into the Popsicle molds and place in freezer for 4 hours or until set.
5. Serve and enjoy.

NUTRITIONS: Calories: 198 Fat: 21 g Carbs: 6 g Sugar: 0.2 g Protein: 3 g Cholesterol: 41 mg

CONCLUSION

The 6 meals Diet has been subjected to various studies to Prove its efficacy in weight loss.

Different studies were Published in various journals indicating that those who follow this Program are able to see significant changes in as little as 8 weeks and that People can achieve their long-term health goals with the 6 meals Diet.

While the initial 5&1 ideal weight Plan is quite restrictive, maintenance Phases 3&3 allow for greater variety of less Processed foods and snacks, which can facilitate weight loss.

Under this diet regimen, dieters are required to follow a weight Plan that includes five fueling a day and one lean green meal daily.

However, there are also other regimens of the Diet if the five fuelings a day is too much for you. And since this is a commercial diet, you have access to coaches and become Part of a community that will encourage you to succeed in your weight loss journey.

Moreover, this diet is also designed for people who want to transition from their old habits to healthier ones.

The diet is a set of three Programs, two of which focus on weight loss and one that is best for weight maintenance, if you are not trying to lose weight. The Plans are high in Protein and low in carbohydrates and calories to stimulate weight loss. Each Program requires you to eat at least half of the food in the form of numerous healthy Prepackaged foods.

Since the Plan requires the intake of carbohydrates, Protein and fat, it is also a relatively balanced Plan when it comes to food groups.

When it comes to weight loss, experts say that while 6 meals diet can help because it is essentially less caloric, it is unlikely to improve your eating habits Permanently.

You are more likely to gain weight after stopping the diet.

Also, diet experts warn that this Pattern may not contain enough calories to meet your body's needs.

"In terms of overall health and nutrition, as well as convenience, this diet isn't at the top of my list of best approaches." she says.

If you are interested in trying this, consider working with an experienced registered dietitian who can help you stay Properly fed as you strive to achieve your desired weight.

For the most desirable 5 and 1 weight Plan, eat 5 foods Per day, Plus a low carb lean meal and a low carb elective snack.

Although Initial Plan 5 & 1 is reasonably restrictive, Protection Segment 3 & 3 allows for a greater variety of less Processed foods and snacks, which can also make weight loss easier and more Persistent for long period.

The bottom line is, that the weight loss Plan Promotes weight loss via low calorie prepackaged meals; low carb homemade food, and Personalized coaching; at the same time, as this system Promotes quick-time Period weight and fat loss, similarly research is wanted to assess whether it encourages the everlasting way of life adjustments needed for long-time Period achievement.

CPSIA information can be obtained
at www.ICGtesting.com
Printed in the USA
BVHW092213080621
609008BV00004B/824

9 781914 045813